PIANO | VOCAL | GUITAR ■ CD   VOLUME 90

Piano Play-Along

IRISH FAVORITES

ISBN 978-1-4234-9116-3

HAL•LEONARD® CORPORATION
7777 W. BLUEMOUND RD. P.O.BOX 13819 MILWAUKEE, WI 53213

In Australia contact:
Hal Leonard Australia Pty. Ltd.
4 Lentara Court
Cheltenham, Victoria, 3192 Australia
Email: ausadmin@halleonard.com.au

Visit Hal Leonard Online at
www.halleonard.com

CONTENTS

COCKLES AND MUSSELS
(Molly Malone)

Traditional Irish Folk Song

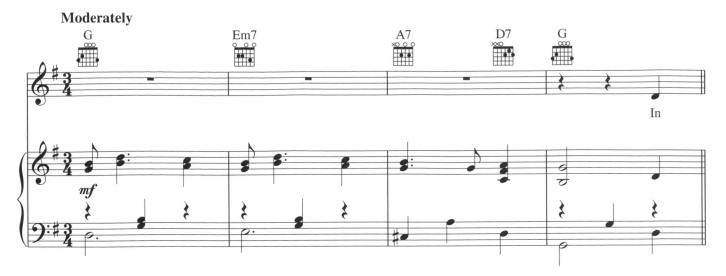

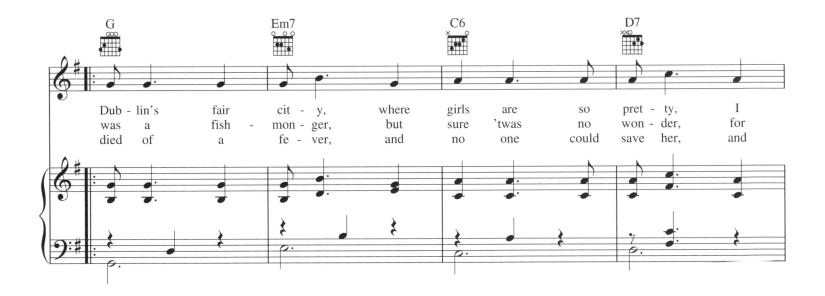

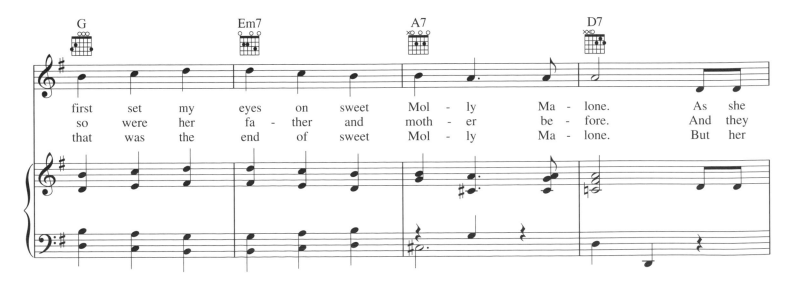

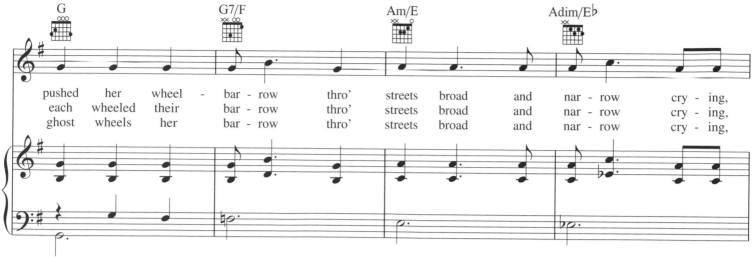

pushed her wheel - bar - row thro' streets broad and nar - row cry - ing,
each wheeled their bar - row thro' streets broad and nar - row cry - ing,
ghost wheels her bar - row thro' streets broad and nar - row cry - ing,

"Cock - les and mus - sels, a - live, a - live, oh!
"Cock - les and mus - sels, a - live, a - live, oh!
"Cock - les and mus - sels, a - live, a - live, oh! A -

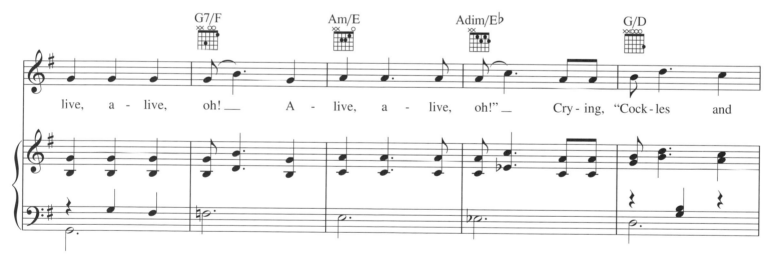

live, a - live, oh! __ A - live, a - live, oh!" __ Cry - ing, "Cock - les and

mus - sels, a - live, a - live, oh!" She oh!"
                                    She

DANNY BOY

Words by FREDERICK EDWARD WEATHERLY
Traditional Irish Folk Melody

back when sum-mer's in the mead - ow, _____ or when the val - ley's hush'd and white with
hear, tho' soft your tread a - bove__ me, _____ and all my dreams will warm and sweet - er

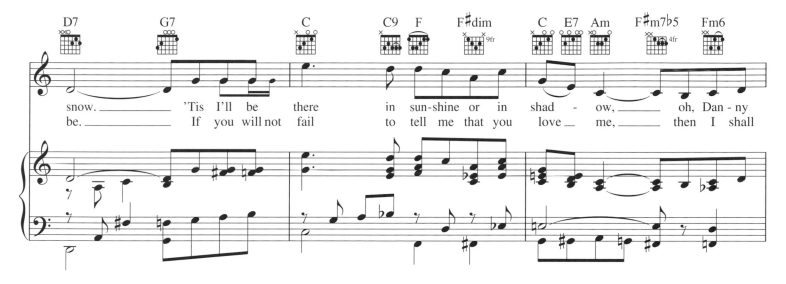

snow. _____ 'Tis I'll be there in sun-shine or in shad - ow, _____ oh, Dan - ny
be. _____ If you will not fail to tell me that you love__ me, _____ then I shall

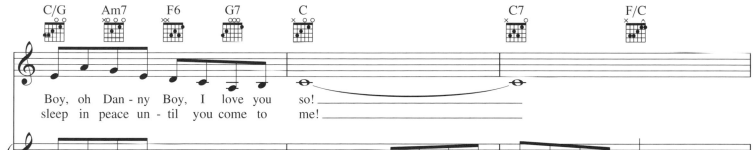

Boy, oh Dan - ny Boy, I love you so! _____
sleep in peace un - til you come to me! _____

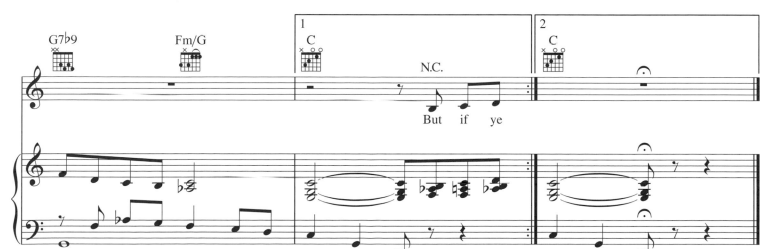

But if ye

I'LL TAKE YOU HOME AGAIN, KATHLEEN

Words and Music by
THOMAS WESTENDORF

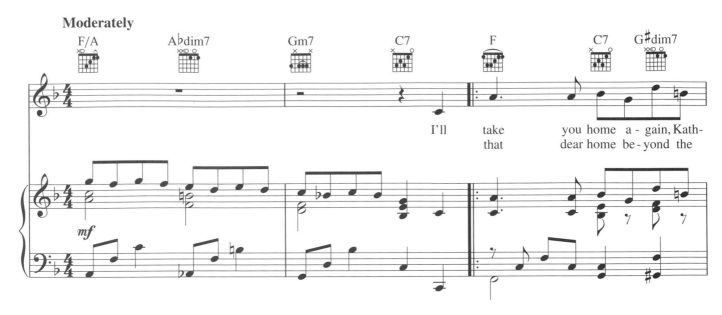

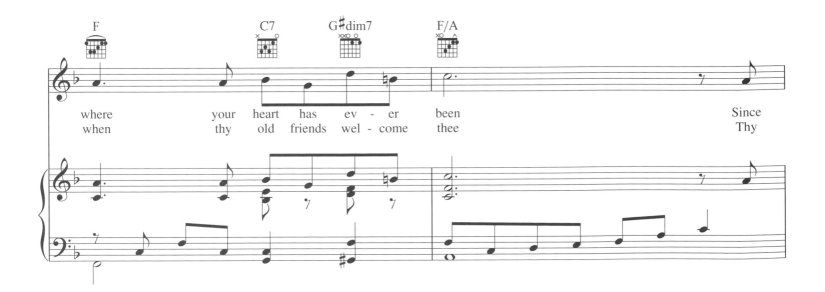

MY WILD IRISH ROSE

Words and Music by
CHAUNCEY OLCOTT

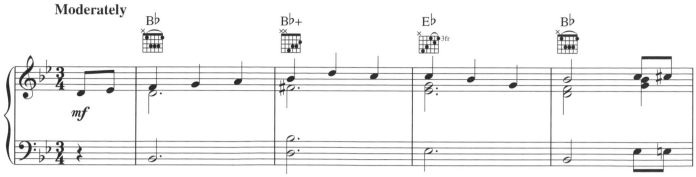

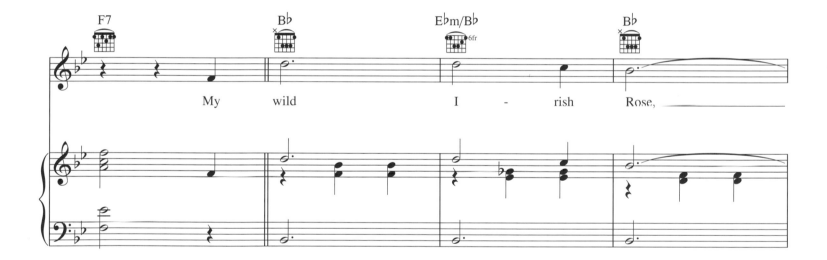

My wild I - rish Rose, _____

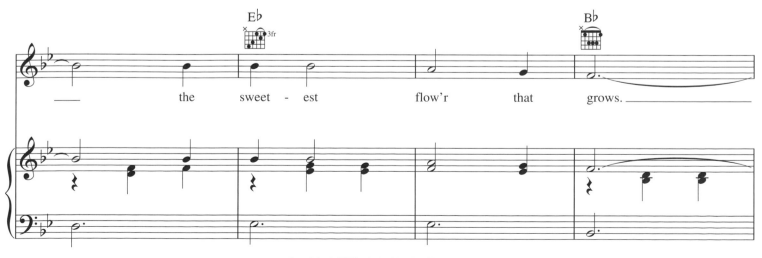

_____ the sweet - est flow'r that grows. _____

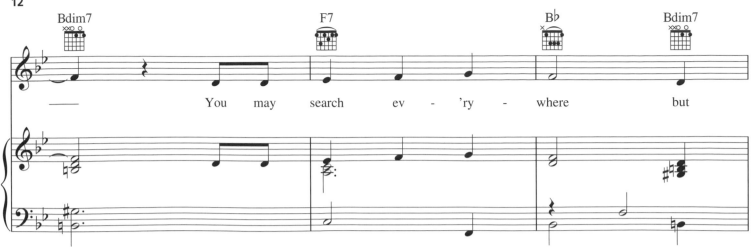

You may search ev - 'ry - where but

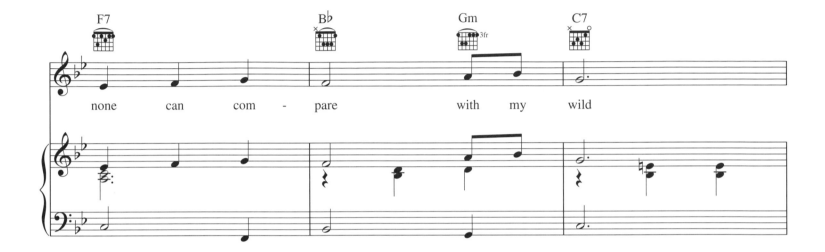

none can com - pare with my wild

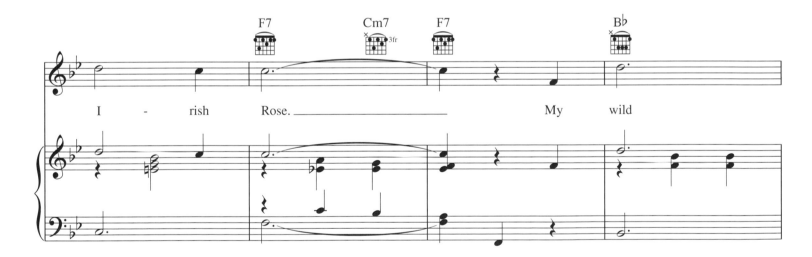

I - rish Rose. _____ My wild

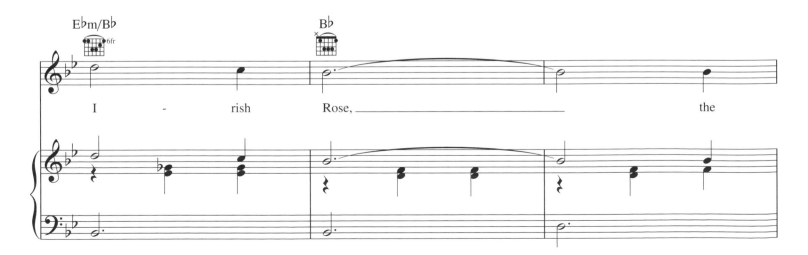

I - rish Rose, _____ the

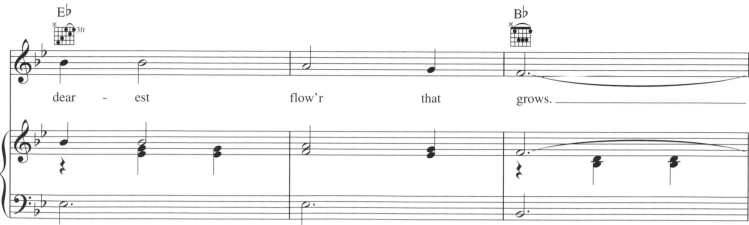

dear - est flow'r that grows. _____

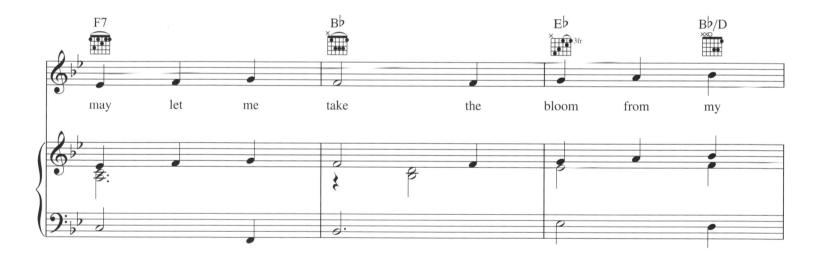

_____ And some day for my sake she

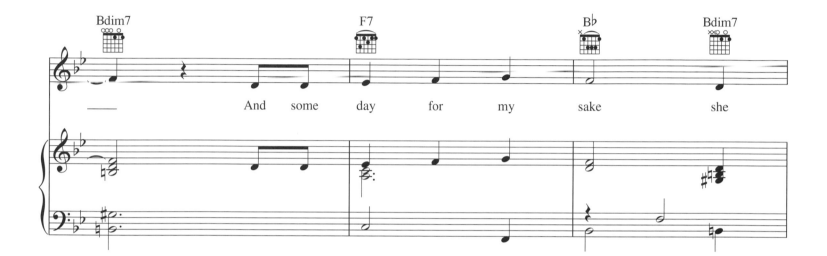

may let me take the bloom from my

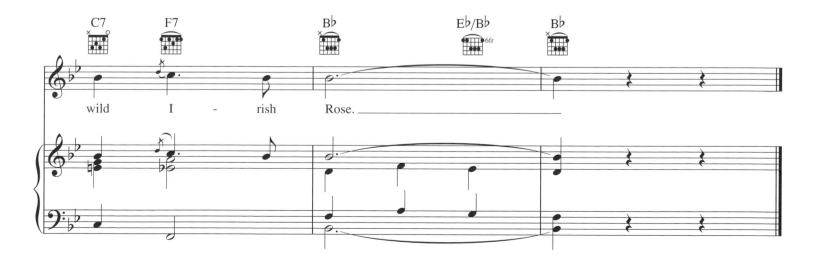

wild I - rish Rose. _____

THE IRISH ROVER

Traditional Irish Folk Song

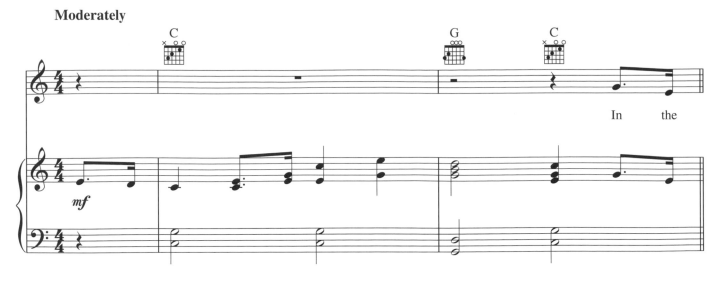

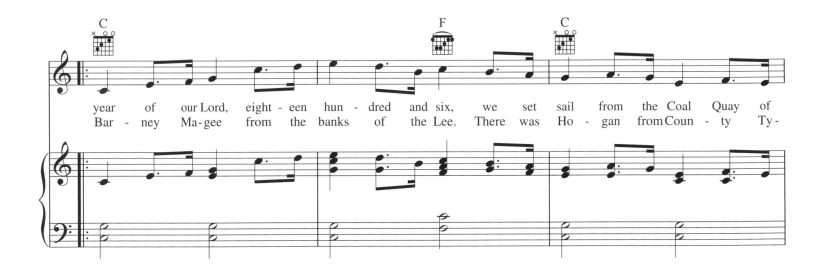

year of our Lord, eight-een hun-dred and six, we set sail from the Coal Quay of
Bar-ney Ma-gee from the banks of the Lee. There was Ho-gan from Coun-ty Ty-

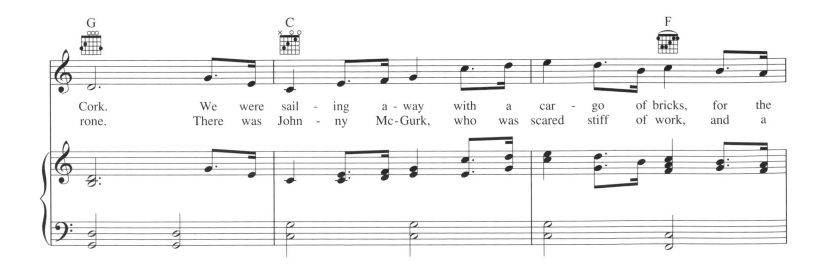

Cork.   We were sail-ing a-way with a car-go of bricks, for the
rone.   There was John-ny Mc-Gurk, who was scared stiff of work, and a

grand cit - y hall in New York. We'd an el - e - gant craft, it was
chap from West-meath named Ma - lone. There was Slug - ger O'-Toole, who was

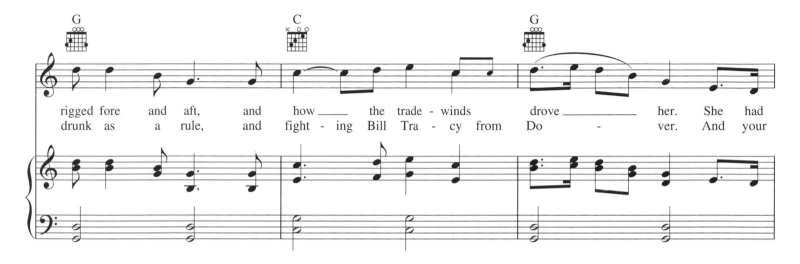

rigged fore and aft, and how _____ the trade - winds drove _____ her. She had
drunk as a rule, and fight - ing Bill Tra - cy from Do - ver. And your

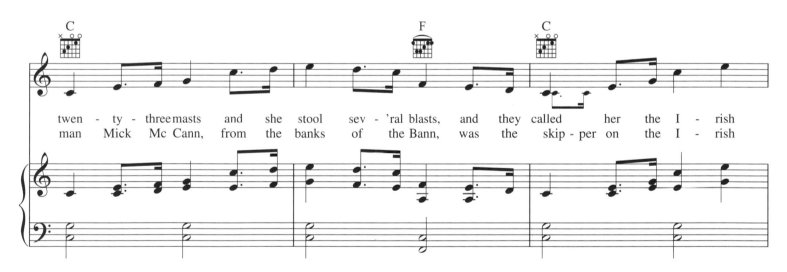

twen - ty - three masts and she stool sev - 'ral blasts, and they called her the I - rish
man Mick Mc Cann, from the banks of the Bann, was the skip - per on the I - rish

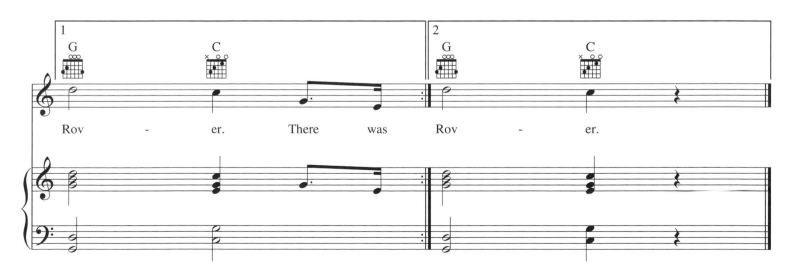

1
Rov - er. There was

2
Rov - er.

MacNAMARA'S BAND

Words by JOHN J. STAMFORD
Music by SHAMUS O'CONNOR

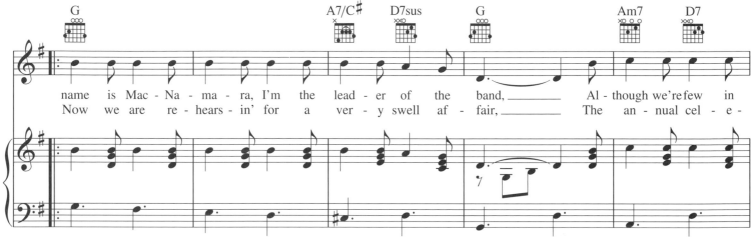

name is Mac-Na-ma-ra, I'm the lead-er of the band,_____ Al-though we're few in
Now we are re-hears-in' for a ver-y swell af-fair,_____ The an-nual cel-e-

num-ber, we're the fin-est in the land. We play at wakes and wed-dings and at
bra-tion, all the gen-try will be there. When Gen-'ral Grant to Ire-land came he

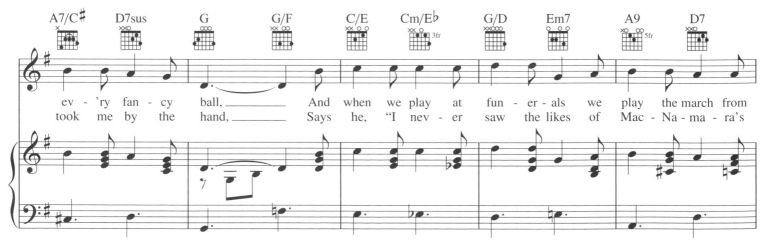

ev'-ry fan-cy ball,_____ And when we play at fun-er-als we play the march from
took me by the hand,_____ Says he, "I nev-er saw the likes of Mac-Na-ma-ra's

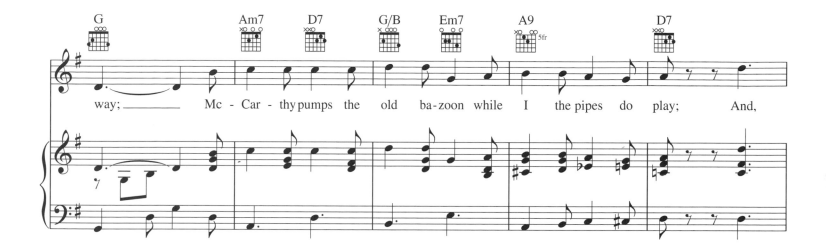

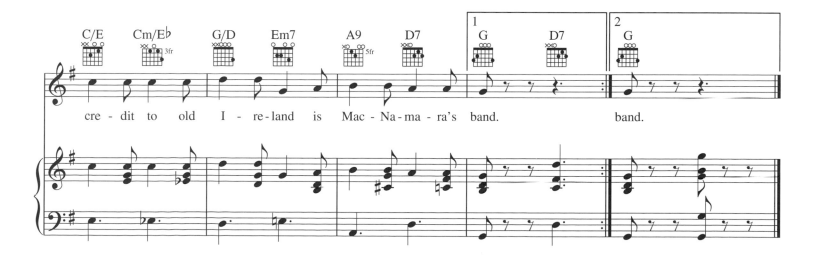

MINSTREL BOY

Traditional

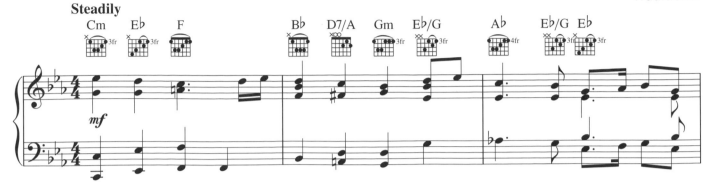

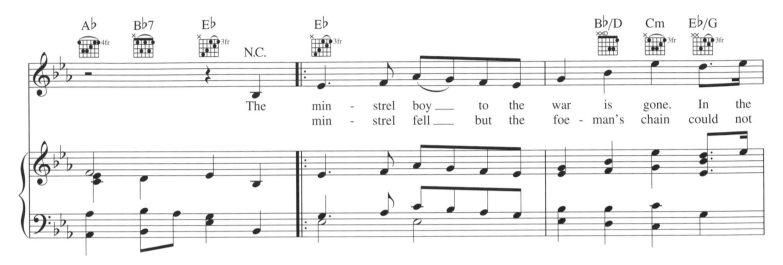

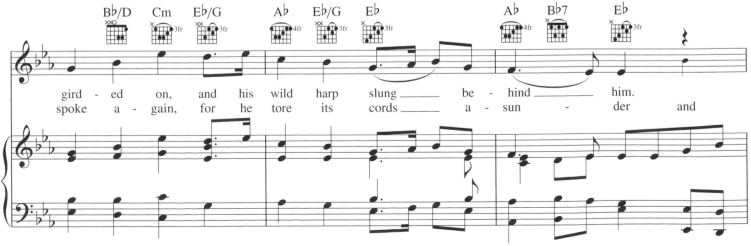

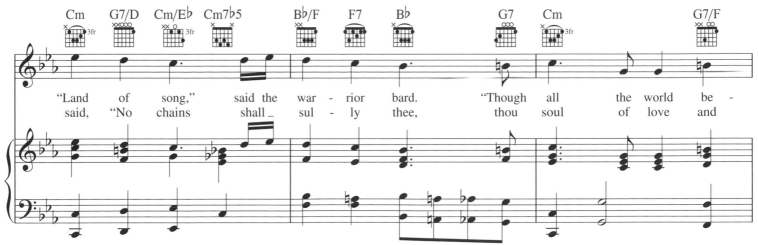

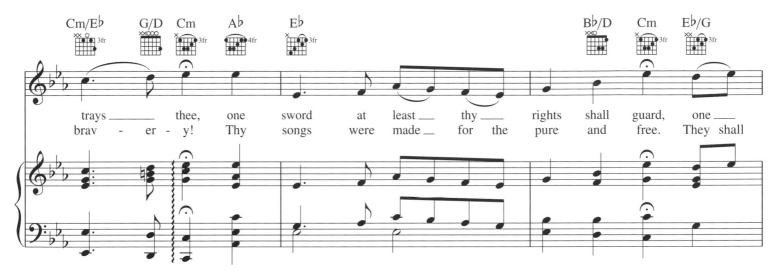

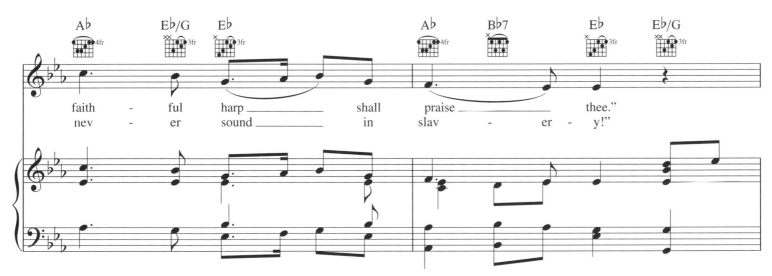

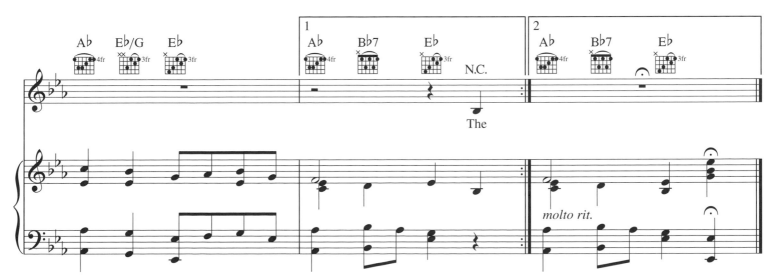

TOO-RA-LOO-RA-LOO-RAL
(That's an Irish Lullaby)

Words and Music by
JAMES R. SHANNON

Moderately

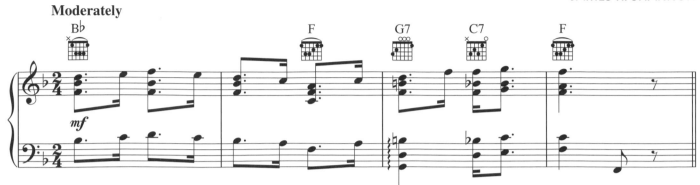

O - ver in Kil - lar - ney, ___ man - y years a - go, me mith - er sang a
Oft, in dreams, I wan - der ___ to that cot a - gain. I feel her arms a

song to me in tones so sweet and low. Just a sim - ple lit - tle dit - ty, in her
hug - gin' me as when she held me then. And I hear her voice a hum - min' to me

good ould I - rish way, and I'd give the world if she could sing that song to me this
as in days of yore when she used to rock me fast a - sleep out - side the cab - in

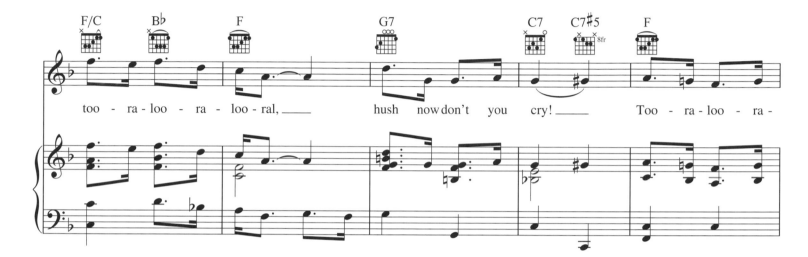

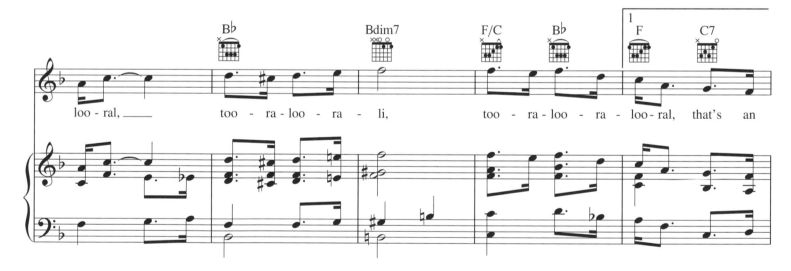

THE WEARING OF THE GREEN

18th Century Irish Folk Song

Oh __ Pad - dy dear, and did you hear the
Then __ since the col - or we must wear is
But, __ if at last our col - or should be

news that's go - ing 'round? The sham - rock is for - bid by law to grow on I - rish
Eng - land's cru - el red, sure Ire - land's sons will ne'er for - get the blood that they have
torn from Ire - land's heart, her sons, with shame and sor - row, from the dear old soil will

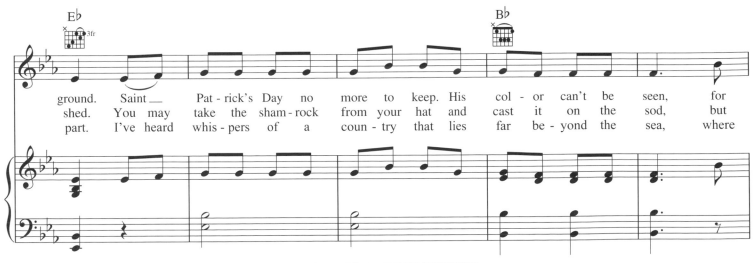

ground. Saint __ Pat - rick's Day no more to keep. His col - or can't be seen, for
shed. You may take the sham - rock from your hat and cast it on the sod, but
part. I've heard whis - pers of a coun - try that lies far be - yond the sea, where

WHEN IRISH EYES ARE SMILING

Words by CHAUNCEY OLCOTT
and GEORGE GRAFF, JR.
Music by ERNEST R. BALL

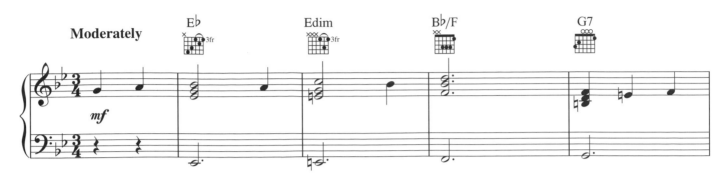

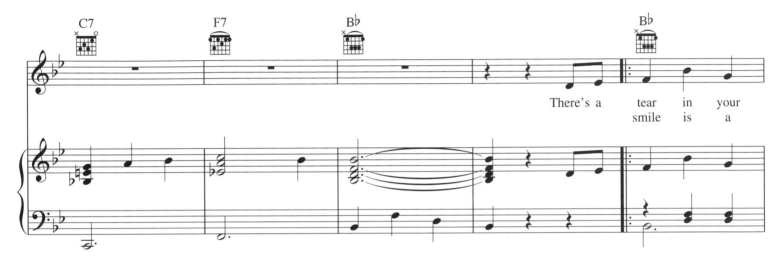

26

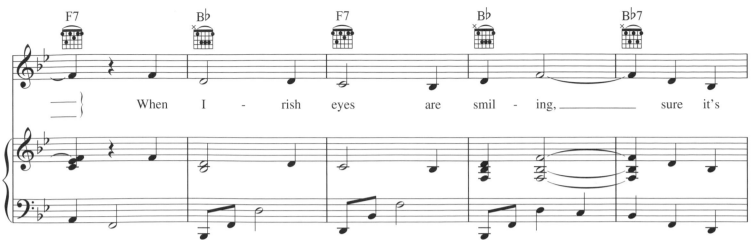

When I - rish eyes are smil - ing, _____ sure it's

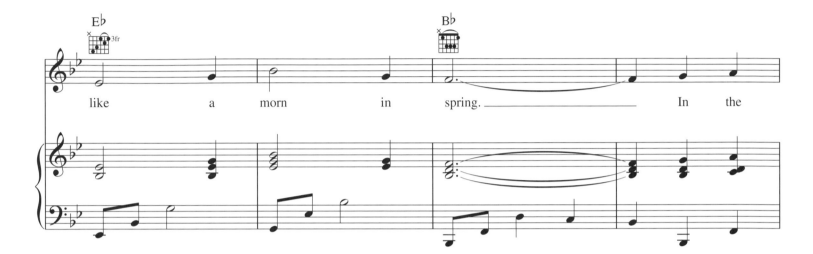

like a morn in spring. _____ In the

lilt of I - rish laugh - ter, you can

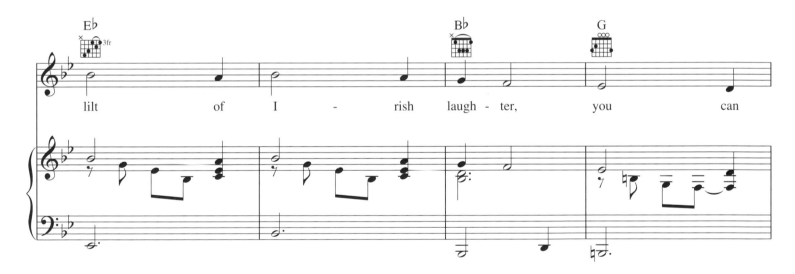

hear the an - gels sing. _____ When

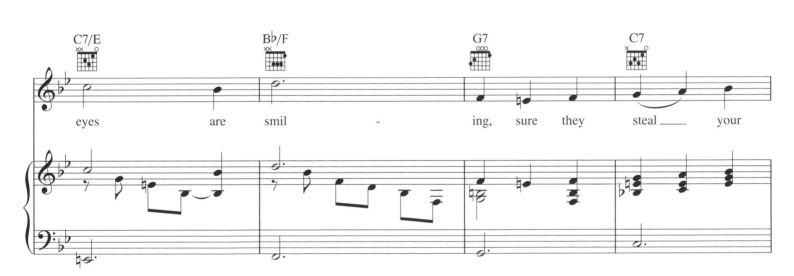

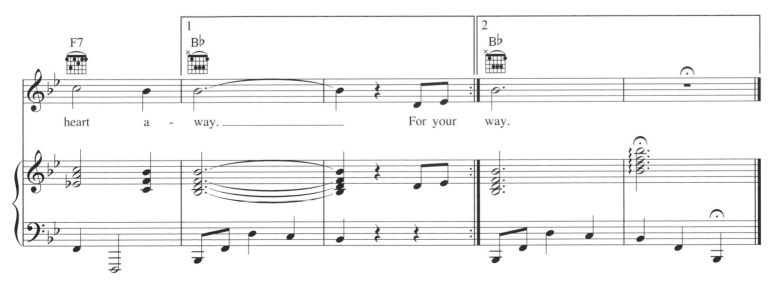

THE ULTIMATE SONGBOOKS

HAL·LEONARD

These great songbook/CD packs come with our standard arrangements for piano and voice with guitar chord frames plus a CD. The CD includes a full performance of each song, as well as a second track without the piano part so you can play "lead" with the band!

1. MOVIE MUSIC
Come What May • My Heart Will Go On (Love Theme from *Titanic*) • The Rainbow Connection • and more.
00311072 P/V/G................$14.95

2. JAZZ BALLADS
Georgia on My Mind • In a Sentimental Mood • The Nearness of You • The Very Thought of You • When Sunny Gets Blue • and more.
00311073 P/V/G................$14.95

3. TIMELESS POP
Ebony and Ivory • Every Breath You Take • From a Distance • I Write the Songs • In My Room • Let It Be • Oh, Pretty Woman • We've Only Just Begun.
00311074 P/V/G................$14.95

4. BROADWAY CLASSICS
Ain't Misbehavin' • Cabaret • If I Were a Bell • Memory • Oklahoma • Some Enchanted Evening • The Sound of Music • You'll Never Walk Alone.
00311075 P/V/G................$14.95

5. DISNEY
Beauty and the Beast • Can You Feel the Love Tonight • A Whole New World • You'll Be in My Heart • You've Got a Friend in Me • and more.
00311076 P/V/G................$14.95

6. COUNTRY STANDARDS
Blue Eyes Crying in the Rain • Crazy • King of the Road • Oh, Lonesome Me • Ring of Fire • Tennessee Waltz • You Are My Sunshine • Your Cheatin' Heart.
00311077 P/V/G................$14.99

7. LOVE SONGS
Can't Help Falling in Love • Here, There and Everywhere • How Deep Is Your Love • Maybe I'm Amazed • You Are So Beautiful • and more.
00311078 P/V/G................$14.95

8. CLASSICAL THEMES
Can Can • Habanera • Humoresque • In the Hall of the Mountain King • Minuet in G Major • Symphony No. 5 in C Minor, 1st Movement Excerpt • and more.
00311079 Piano Solo................$14.95

9. CHILDREN'S SONGS
Do-Re-Mi • It's a Small World • Linus and Lucy • Sesame Street Theme • Sing • Winnie the Pooh • Won't You Be My Neighbor? • Yellow Submarine.
0311080 P/V/G................$14.95

10. WEDDING CLASSICS
Air on the G String • Ave Maria • Bridal Chorus • Canon in D • Jesu, Joy of Man's Desiring • Ode to Joy • Trumpet Voluntary • Wedding March.
00311081 Piano Solo................$14.95

11. WEDDING FAVORITES
All I Ask of You • Don't Know Much • Endless Love • Grow Old with Me • In My Life • Longer • Wedding Processional • You and I.
00311097 P/V/G................$14.95

12. CHRISTMAS FAVORITES
Blue Christmas • The Christmas Song • Do You Hear What I Hear • Here Comes Santa Claus • Merry Christmas, Darling • Silver Bells • and more.
00311137 P/V/G................$15.95

13. YULETIDE FAVORITES
Away in a Manger • Deck the Hall • The First Noel • Go, Tell It on the Mountain • Jingle Bells • Joy to the World • O Little Town of Bethlehem • and more.
00311138 P/V/G................$14.95

14. POP BALLADS
Have I Told You Lately • I'll Be There for You • Rainy Days and Monday • She's Got a Way • Your Song • and more.
00311145 P/V/G................$14.95

15. FAVORITE STANDARDS
Call Me • The Girl from Ipanema • Moon River • My Way • Satin Doll • Smoke Gets in Your Eyes • Strangers in the Night • The Way You Look Tonight.
00311146 P/V/G................$14.95

16. TV CLASSICS
The Brady Bunch • Green Acres Theme • Happy Days • Johnny's Theme • Love Boat Theme • Mister Ed • The Munsters Theme • Where Everybody Knows Your Name.
00311147 P/V/G................$14.95

17. MOVIE FAVORITES
Back to the Future • Theme from E.T. • Footloose • Somewhere in Time • Somewhere Out There • and more.
00311148 P/V/G................$14.95

18. JAZZ STANDARDS
All the Things You Are • Bluesette • Easy Living • I'll Remember April • Isn't It Romantic? • Stella by Starlight • Tangerine • Yesterdays.
00311149 P/V/G................$14.95

19. CONTEMPORARY HITS
Beautiful • Calling All Angels • Don't Know Why • If I Ain't Got You • 100 Years • This Love • A Thousand Miles • You Raise Me Up.
00311162 P/V/G................$14.95

20. R&B BALLADS
After the Love Has Gone • All in Love Is Fair • Hello • I'll Be There • Let's Stay Together • Midnight Train to Georgia • Tell It like It Is • Three Times a Lady.
00311163 P/V/G................$14.95

21. BIG BAND
All or Nothing at All • Apple Honey • April in Paris • Cherokee • In the Mood • Opus One • Stardust • Stompin' at the Savoy.
00311164 P/V/G................$14.95

22. ROCK CLASSICS
Against All Odds • Bennie and the Jets • Come Sail Away • Do It Again • Free Bird • Jump • Wanted Dead or Alive • We Are the Champions.
00311165 P/V/G................$14.95

23. WORSHIP CLASSICS
Awesome God • Lord, Be Glorified • Lord, I Lift Your Name on High • Shine, Jesus, Shine • Step by Step • There Is a Redeemer • and more.
00311166 P/V/G................$14.95

24. LES MISÉRABLES
Bring Him Home • Castle on a Cloud • Empty Chairs at Empty Tables • I Dreamed a Dream • A Little Fall of Rain • On My Own • and more.
00311169 P/V/G................$14.95

25. THE SOUND OF MUSIC
Climb Ev'ry Mountain • Do-Re-Mi • Edelweiss • Maria • My Favorite Things • Sixteen Going on Seventeen • Something Good • The Sound of Music.
00311175 P/V/G................$15.99

26. ANDREW LLOYD WEBBER FAVORITES
All I Ask of You • Amigos Para Siempre • As If We Never Said Goodbye • Everything's Alright • Memory • No Matter What • Tell Me on a Sunday • You Must Love Me.
00311178 P/V/G................$14.95

27. ANDREW LLOYD WEBBER GREATS
Don't Cry for Me Argentina • I Don't Know How to Love Him • The Phantom of the Opera • Whistle down the Wind • With One Look • and more.
00311179 P/V/G................$14.95

28. LENNON & MCCARTNEY
Eleanor Rigby • Hey Jude • The Long and Winding Road • Love Me Do • Lucy in the Sky with Diamonds • Nowhere Man • Strawberry Fields Forever • Yesterday.
00311180 P/V/G................$14.95

29. THE BEACH BOYS
Barbara Ann • Be True to Your School • California Girls • Fun, Fun, Fun • Help Me Rhonda • I Get Around • Little Deuce Coupe • Wouldn't It Be Nice.
00311181 P/V/G................$14.95

30. ELTON JOHN
Candle in the Wind • Crocodile Rock • Daniel • Goodbye Yellow Brick Road • I Guess That's Why They Call It the Blues • Levon • Your Song • and more.
00311182 P/V/G................$14.95

31. CARPENTERS
(They Long to Be) Close to You • Only Yesterday • Rainy Days and Mondays • Top of the World • We've Only Just Begun • Yesterday Once More • and more.
00311183 P/V/G................$14.95

32. BACHARACH & DAVID
Alfie • Do You Know the Way to San Jose • The Look of Love • Raindrops Keep Fallin' on My Head • What the World Needs Now Is Love • and more.
00311218 P/V/G................$14.95

33. PEANUTS™
Blue Charlie Brown • Charlie Brown Theme • The Great Pumpkin Waltz • Joe Cool • Linus and Lucy • Oh, Good Grief • Red Baron • You're in Love, Charlie Brown.
00311227 P/V/G................$14.95

34 CHARLIE BROWN CHRISTMAS
Christmas Is Coming • The Christmas Song • Christmas Time Is Here • Linus and Lucy • My Little Drum • O Tannenbaum • Skating • What Child Is This.
00311228 P/V/G................$15.95

35. ELVIS PRESLEY HITS
Blue Suede Shoes • Can't Help Falling in Love • Heartbreak Hotel • Love Me • (Let Me Be Your) Teddy Bear and more.
00311230 P/V/G................$14.95

36. ELVIS PRESLEY GREATS
All Shook Up • Don't • Jailhouse Rock • Love Me Tender • Loving You • Return to Sender • Too Much • Wooden Heart.
00311231 P/V/G................$14.95

37. CONTEMPORARY CHRISTIAN
El Shaddai • Every Season • Here I Am • Jesus Will Still Be There • Let Us Pray • Place in This World • Who Am I • Wisdom.
00311232 P/V/G................$14.95

38. DUKE ELLINGTON STANDARDS
Caravan • I Got It Bad and That Ain't Good • In a Sentimental Mood • Love You Madly • Mood Indigo • Sophisticated Lady • more.
00311233 P/V/G................$14.95

39. DUKE ELLINGTON CLASSICS
Don't Get Around Much Anymore • I Let a Song Go out of My Heart • In a Mellow Tone • Satin Doll • Take the "A" Train • and more.
00311234 P/V/G................$14.95

40. SHOWTUNES
The Best of Times • Hello, Dolly! • I'll Know • Mame • Summer Nights • Till There Was You • Tomorrow • What I Did for Love.
00311237 P/V/G................$14.95

41. RODGERS & HAMMERSTEIN
Bali Ha'i • Hello, Young Lovers • If I Loved You • It Might as Well Be Spring • Love, Look Away • Oh, What a Beautiful Mornin' • and more.
00311238 P/V/G................$14.95

42. IRVING BERLIN
Always • Blue Skies • Change Partners • Cheek to Cheek • Easter Parade • How Deep Is the Ocean (How High Is the Sky) • Puttin' on the Ritz • What'll I Do?
00311239 P/V/G................$14.95

43. JEROME KERN
Can't Help Lovin' Dat Man • A Fine Romance • I Won't Dance • I'm Old Fashioned • The Last Time I Saw Paris • Ol' Man River • and more.
00311240 P/V/G................$14.95

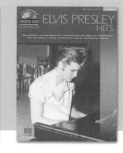

44. FRANK SINATRA – POPULAR HITS
Come Fly with Me • Cycles • High Hopes • Love and Marriage • My Way • Strangers in the Night • (Love Is) The Tender Trap • Young at Heart.
00311277 P/V/G $14.95

45. FRANK SINATRA – MOST REQUESTED SONGS
From Here to Eternity • I've Got the World on a String • Theme from "New York, New York" • Night and Day • Time After Time • Witchcraft • and more.
00311278 P/V/G $14.95

46. WICKED
Dancing Through Life • Defying Gravity • For Good • I Couldn't Be Happier • I'm Not That Girl • Popular • What Is This Feeling? • The Wizard and I.
00311317 P/V/G $15.99

47. RENT
I'll Cover You • Light My Candle • One Song Glory • Out Tonight • Rent • Seasons of Love • What You Own • Without You.
00311319 P/V/G $14.95

48. CHRISTMAS CAROLS
God Rest Ye Merry, Gentlemen • Hark! the Herald Angels Sing • It Came upon the Midnight Clear • O Holy Night • Silent Night • What Child Is This? • and more.
00311332 P/V/G $14.95

49. HOLIDAY HITS
Frosty the Snow Man • Happy Xmas (War Is Over) • I'll Be Home for Christmas • Jingle-Bell Rock • Rudolph the Red-Nosed Reindeer • Santa Claus Is Comin' to Town • and more.
00311333 P/V/G $14.95

50. DISNEY CLASSICS
Some Day My Prince Will Come • When You Wish upon a Star • Whistle While You Work • Who's Afraid of the Big Bad Wolf? • Zip-A-Dee-Doo-Dah • and more.
00311417 P/V/G $14.95

51. HIGH SCHOOL MUSICAL
9 songs, including: Breaking Free • Get'cha Head in the Game • Start of Something New • We're All in This Together • What I've Been Looking For • and more.
00311421 P/V/G $19.95

52. ANDREW LLOYD WEBBER CLASSICS
Another Suitcase in Another Hall • Close Every Door • Love Changes Everything • Pie Jesu • Wishing You Were Somehow Here Again • more.
00311422 P/V/G $14.95

53. GREASE
Beauty School Dropout • Grease • Greased Lightnin' • Hopelessly Devoted to You • Sandy • Summer Nights • You're the One That I Want • and more.
00311450 P/V/G $14.95

54. BROADWAY FAVORITES
Big Spender • Comedy Tonight • Hello, Young Lovers • I've Grown Accustomed to Her Face • Just in Time • Make Someone Happy • My Ship • People.
00311451 P/V/G $14.95

55. THE 1940S
Come Rain or Come Shine • It Could Happen to You • Moonlight in Vermont • A Nightingale Sang in Berkeley Square • Route 66 • Sentimental Journey • and more.
00311453 P/V/G $14.95

56. THE 1950S
Blueberry Hill • Dream Lover • Fever • The Great Pretender • Kansas City • Memories Are Made of This • My Prayer • Put Your Head on My Shoulder.
00311459 P/V/G $14.95

57. THE 1960S
Beyond the Sea • Blue Velvet • California Dreamin' • Downtown • For Once in My Life • Let's Hang On • (Sittin' On) The Dock of the Bay • The Twist.
00311460 P/V/G $14.99

58. THE 1970S
Dust in the Wind • Everything Is Beautiful • How Can You Mend a Broken Heart • I Feel the Earth Move • If • Joy to the World • My Eyes Adored You • You've Got a Friend.
00311461 P/V/G $14.99

59. THE 1980S
All Night Long (All Night) • Another One Bites the Dust • Every Little Thing She Does Is Magic • Got My Mind Set on You • I Just Called to Say I Love You • Kokomo • Saving All My Love for You • Stand by Me.
00311462 P/V/G $14.99

60. THE 1990S
Don't Speak • (Everything I Do) I Do It for You • Hero • I Believe I Can Fly • I Don't Want to Wait • I'll Be • Save the Best for Last • Walking in Memphis.
00311463 P/V/G $14.99

61. BILLY JOEL FAVORITES
And So It Goes • Baby Grand • It's Still Rock and Roll to Me • Leave a Tender Moment Alone • Piano Man • She's Always a Woman • Uptown Girl • You May Be Right.
00311464 P/V/G $14.95

62. BILLY JOEL HITS
The Entertainer • Honesty • Just the Way You Are • The Longest Time • Lullabye (Goodnight, My Angel) • My Life • New York State of Mind • She's Got a Way.
00311465 P/V/G $14.95

63. HIGH SCHOOL MUSICAL 2
All for One • Everyday • Fabulous • Gotta Go My Own Way • I Don't Dance • What Time Is It • Work This Out • You Are the Music in Me.
00311470 P/V/G $19.95

64. GOD BLESS AMERICA
America • America, the Beautiful • Anchors Aweigh • Battle Hymn of the Republic • God Bless America • This Is My Country • This Land Is Your Land • and more.
00311489 P/V/G $14.95

65. CASTING CROWNS
Does Anybody Hear Her • East to West • Here I Go Again • Praise You in This Storm • Somewhere in the Middle • Voice of Truth • While You Were Sleeping • Who Am I.
00311494 P/V/G $14.95

66. HANNAH MONTANA
I Got Nerve • Just like You • Life's What You Make It • Nobody's Perfect• Old Blue Jeans • Pumpin' up the Party • Rock Star • We Got the Party.
00311772 P/V/G $19.95

67. BROADWAY GEMS
Getting to Know You • I Could Have Danced All Night • If I Were a Rich Man • It's a Lovely Day Today • September Song • The Song Is You • and more.
00311803 P/V/G $14.99

68. LENNON & McCARTNEY FAVORITES
All My Loving • The Fool on the Hill • A Hard Day's Night • Here, There and Everywhere • I Saw Her Standing There • Yellow Submarine • and more.
00311804 P/V/G $14.99

69. PIRATES OF THE CARIBBEAN
All for One • Everyday • Fabulous • Gotta Go My Own Way • I Don't Dance • What Time Is It • Work This Out • You Are the Music in Me.
00311807 P/V/G $14.95

70. "TOMORROW," "PUT ON A HAPPY FACE," AND OTHER CHARLES STROUSE HITS
Born Too Late • A Lot of Livin' to Do • Night Song • Once upon a Time • Put on a Happy Face • Those Were the Days • Tomorrow • You've Got Possibilities.
00311821 P/V/G $14.99

71. ROCK BAND
Black Hole Sun • Don't Fear the Reaper • Learn to Fly • Paranoid • Say It Ain't So • Suffragette City • Wanted Dead or Alive • Won't Get Fooled Again.
00311822 P/V/G $14.99

72. HIGH SCHOOL MUSICAL 3
Can I Have This Dance • High School Musical • I Want It All • A Night to Remember • Now or Never • Right Here Right Now • Scream • Walk Away.
00311826 P/V/G $19.99

73. MAMMA MIA! – THE MOVIE
Dancing Queen • Gimme! Gimme! Gimme! (A Man After Midnight) • Honey, Honey • Lay All Your Love on Me • Mamma Mia • SOS • Take a Chance on Me • The Winner Takes It All.
00311831 P/V/G $14.99

75. TWILIGHT
Bella's Lullaby • Decode • Full Moon • Go All the Way (Into the Twilight) • Spotlight (Twilight Remix) • Supermassive Black Hole • Tremble for My Beloved.
00311860 P/V/G $16.99

76. PRIDE & PREJUDICE
Arrival at Netherfield • Darcy's Letter • Dawn • Georgiana • Leaving Netherfield • The Living Sculptures of Pemberley • Meryton Townhall • The Secret Life of Daydreams.
00311862 P/V/G $14.99

77. ELTON JOHN FAVORITES
Bennie and the Jets • Blue Eyes • Don't Go Breaking My Heart • Don't Let the Sun Go down on Me • Rocket Man (I Think It's Gonna Be a Long Long Time) • Sacrifice • Someone Saved My Life Tonight • Tiny Dancer.
00311884 P/V/G $14.99

78. ERIC CLAPTON
Bell Bottom Blues • I Can't Stand It • I Shot the Sheriff • Lay Down Sally • Layla • Sunshine of Your Love • Tears in Heaven • Wonderful Tonight.
00311885 P/V/G $14.99

79. TANGOS
Adios Muchachos • Amapola • Aquellos Ojos Verdes • El Choclo • Rose Room • Say "Si, Si" • Takes Two to Tango • Tango of Roses.
00311886 P/V/G $14.99

80. FIDDLER ON THE ROOF
Do You Love Me? • Far from the Home I Love • Fiddler on the Roof • If I Were a Rich Man • Matchmaker • Sabbath Prayer • Sunrise, Sunset • Tradition.
00311887 P/V/G $14.99

81. JOSH GROBAN
February Song • Machine • Now or Never • Per Te • Remember When It Rained • So She Dances • Un Dia Llegara • You Raise Me Up.
00311901 P/V/G $14.99

82. LIONEL RICHIE
All Night Long (All Night) • Lady • Penny Lover • Say You, Say Me • Still • Stuck on You • Three Times a Lady • Truly.
00311902 P/V/G $14.99

83. PHANTOM OF THE OPERA
All I Ask of You • Angel of Music • Masquerade • The Music of the Night • The Phantom of the Opera • The Point of No Return • Think of Me • Wishing You Were Somehow Here Again.
00311903 P/V/G $14.99

84. ANTONIO CARLOS JOBIM FAVORITES
Água De Beber • Chega De Saudade • Dindi • The Girl from Ipanema • Meditation • Quiet Nights of Quiet Stars • Triste • Vivo Sonhando.
00311919 P/V/G $14.99

85. LATIN FAVORITES
Bésame Mucho • A Day in the Life of a Fool • The Look of Love • More • Samba De Orfeu • Sway • Watch What Happens • You Belong to My Heart.
00311920 P/V/G $14.99

89. FAVORITE HYMNS
Beautiful Savior • The Church's One Foundation • Crown Him with Many Crowns • Faith of Our Fathers • Holy, Holy, Holy • A Mighty Fortress Is Our God • My Faith Looks up to Thee • Onward, Christian Soldiers • Rock of Ages • We Gather Together.
00311940 P/V/G $14.99

90. IRISH FAVORITES
Cockles and Mussels (Molly Malone) • Danny Boy • I'll Take You Home Again, Kathleen • The Irish Rover • MacNamara's Band • Minstrel Boy • My Wild Irish Rose • Too-Ra-Loo-Ra-Loo-Ral (That's an Irish Lullaby) • The Wearing of the Green • When Irish Eyes Are Smiling.
00311969 P/V/G $14.99

FOR MORE INFORMATION,
SEE YOUR LOCAL MUSIC DEALER,
OR WRITE TO:

HAL•LEONARD® CORPORATION
7777 W. BLUEMOUND RD. P.O. BOX 13819
MILWAUKEE, WISCONSIN 53213

Visit Hal Leonard Online at
www.halleonard.com

Prices, contents and availability subject to change without notice.

PEANUTS © United Feature Syndicate, Inc.

0110

Big Books of Music

Our "Big Books" feature big selections of popular titles under one cover, perfect for performing musicians, music aficionados or the serious hobbyist. All books are arranged for piano, voice, and guitar, and feature stay-open binding, so the books lie flat without breaking the spine.

BIG BOOK OF BALLADS
62 songs.
00310485 ....$19.95

BIG BOOK OF BIG BAND HITS
84 songs.
00310701 ....$19.95

BIG BOOK OF BLUEGRASS SONGS
70 songs.
00311484 ....$19.95

BIG BOOK OF BLUES
80 songs.
00311843 ....$19.99

BIG BOOK OF BROADWAY
70 songs.
00311658 ....$19.95

BIG BOOK OF CHILDREN'S SONGS
55 songs.
00359261 ....$14.95

GREAT BIG BOOK OF CHILDREN'S SONGS
76 songs.
00310002 ....$14.95

FANTASTIC BIG BOOK OF CHILDREN'S SONGS
66 songs.
00311062 ....$17.95

MIGHTY BIG BOOK OF CHILDREN'S SONGS
65 songs.
00310467 ....$14.95

REALLY BIG BOOK OF CHILDREN'S SONGS
63 songs.
00310372 ....$16.95

BIG BOOK OF CHILDREN'S MOVIE SONGS
66 songs.
00310731 ....$19.95

BIG BOOK OF CHRISTMAS SONGS
126 songs.
00311520 ....$19.95

BIG BOOK OF CLASSIC ROCK
77 songs.
00310801 ....$22.95

BIG BOOK OF CLASSICAL MUSIC
100 songs.
00310508 ....$19.95

BIG BOOK OF CONTEMPORARY CHRISTIAN FAVORITES
50 songs.
00310021 ....$19.95

BIG BOOK OF COUNTRY MUSIC
63 songs.
00310188 ....$19.95

BIG BOOK OF COUNTRY ROCK
64 songs.
00311748 ....$19.99

BIG BOOK OF DISCO & FUNK
70 songs.
00310878 ....$19.95

BIG BOOK OF EARLY ROCK N' ROLL
99 songs.
00310398 ....$19.95

BIG BOOK OF '50S & '60S SWINGING SONGS
67 songs.
00310982 ....$19.95

BIG BOOK OF FOLK POP ROCK
79 songs.
00311125 ....$24.95

BIG BOOK OF FRENCH SONGS
70 songs.
00311154 ....$19.95

BIG BOOK OF GOSPEL SONGS
100 songs.
00310604 ....$19.95

BIG BOOK OF HYMNS
125 hymns.
00310510 ....$17.95

BIG BOOK OF IRISH SONGS
76 songs.
00310981 ....$19.95

BIG BOOK OF ITALIAN FAVORITES
80 songs.
00311185 ....$19.95

BIG BOOK OF JAZZ
75 songs.
00311557 ....$19.95

BIG BOOK OF LATIN AMERICAN SONGS
89 songs.
00311562 ....$19.95

BIG BOOK OF LOVE SONGS
80 songs.
00310784 ....$19.95

BIG BOOK OF MOTOWN
84 songs.
00311061 ....$19.95

BIG BOOK OF MOVIE MUSIC
72 songs.
00311582 ....$19.95

BIG BOOK OF NOSTALGIA
158 songs.
00310004 ....$19.95

BIG BOOK OF OLDIES
73 songs.
00310756 ....$19.95

BIG BOOK OF RAGTIME PIANO
63 songs.
00311749 ....$19.95

BIG BOOK OF RHYTHM & BLUES
67 songs.
00310169 ....$19.95

BIG BOOK OF ROCK
78 songs.
00311566 ....$22.95

BIG BOOK OF SOUL
71 songs.
00310771 ....$19.95

BIG BOOK OF STANDARDS
86 songs.
00311667 ....$19.95

BIG BOOK OF SWING
84 songs.
00310359 ....$19.95

BIG BOOK OF TORCH SONGS
75 songs.
00310561 ....$19.95

BIG BOOK OF TV THEME SONGS
78 songs.
00310504 ....$19.95

BIG BOOK OF WEDDING MUSIC
77 songs.
00311567 ....$19.95

THE BEST EVER
COLLECTION
ARRANGED FOR PIANO, VOICE AND GUITAR

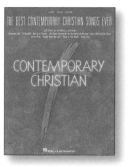

150 of the Most Beautiful Songs Ever
150 ballads
00360735 ....$24.95

150 More of the Most Beautiful Songs Ever
150 songs
00311318.................................$24.95

Best Acoustic Rock Songs Ever
65 acoustic hits
00310984 ....$19.95

Best Big Band Songs Ever
68 big band hits
00359129 ....$16.95

Best Broadway Songs Ever
83 songs
00309155 ....$24.95

More of the Best Broadway Songs Ever
82 songs
00311501 ....$22.95

Best Children's Songs Ever
102 tunes
00310360 (Easy Piano) $19.95

Best Christmas Songs Ever
69 holiday favorites
00359130 ....$19.95

Best Classic Rock Songs Ever
64 hits
00310800 ....$19.99

Best Classical Music Ever
86 classical favorites
00310674 (Piano Solo) $19.95

Best Contemporary Christian Songs Ever
50 favorites
00310558 ....$19.95

Best Country Songs Ever
78 classic country hits
00359135 ....$19.95

Best Early Rock 'n' Roll Songs Ever
74 songs
00310816 ....$19.95

Best Easy Listening Songs Ever
75 mellow favorites
00359193 ....$19.95

Best Gospel Songs Ever
80 gospel songs
00310503 ....$19.95

Best Hymns Ever
118 hymns
00310774 ....$18.95

Best Jazz Standards Ever
77 jazz hits
00311641 ....$19.95

More of the Best Jazz Standards Ever
74 beloved jazz hits
00311023 ....$19.95

Best Latin Songs Ever
67 songs
00310355 ....$19.95

Best Love Songs Ever
65 favorite love songs
00359198 ....$19.95

Best Movie Songs Ever
74 songs
00310063 ....$19.95

Best Praise & Worship Songs Ever
80 all-time favorites
00311057 ....$19.95

More of the Best Praise & Worship Songs Ever
80 songs
00311800 ....$19.99

Best R&B Songs Ever
66 songs
00310184 ....$19.95

Best Rock Songs Ever
63 songs
00490424 ....$18.95

Best Songs Ever
72 must-own classics
00359224 ....$22.95

More of the Best Songs Ever
79 more favorites
00310437 ....$19.95

Best Soul Songs Ever
70 hits
00311427 ....$19.95

Best Standards Ever, Vol. 1 (A-L)
72 beautiful ballads
00359231 ....$17.95

More of the Best Standards Ever, Vol. 1 (A-L)
76 all-time favorites
00310813 ....$17.95

Best Standards Ever, Vol. 2 (M-Z)
72 songs
00359232 ....$17.95

More of the Best Standards Ever, Vol. 2 (M-Z)
75 stunning standards
00310814 ....$17.95

Best Torch Songs Ever
70 sad and sultry favorites
00311027 ....$19.95

Best TV Songs Ever
64 catchy theme songs
00311048 ....$17.95

Best Wedding Songs Ever
70 songs
00311096 ....$19.95

FOR MORE INFORMATION, SEE YOUR LOCAL MUSIC DEALER,
OR WRITE TO:

HAL•LEONARD®
CORPORATION
7777 W. BLUEMOUND RD. P.O. BOX 13819 MILWAUKEE, WI 53213

Visit us on-line for complete songlists at
www.halleonard.com

Prices, contents and availability subject to change without
notice. Not all products available outside the U.S.A.

0309